Drew Posada

Dieses Buch ist jenen Menschen gewidmet, die mich unterstützten
und mir geholfen haben – ein Künstler zu werden...

Kip Curington,
Dennis Presley, Phillip Bradshaw
Tante Helene Alexandra, Brian Haberlin, Dr. Hy Algazi
Joe Antonelli, Princess Dawn
&
die größte Hilfe von allen, jeden Tag...
meine Katze, Lil Elvis.

Ich danke Euch... ich danke Euch vielmals.

*This book is dedicated to the people that supported and helped me
to become an artist in more ways than they'll ever know...*

*Kip Curington
Dennis Presley, Phillip Bradshaw,
Aunt Helene Alexandra, Brian Haberlin, Dr. Hy Algazi
Joe Antonelli, Princess Dawn
&
the biggest helper of all, on a daily basis....
my cat, Lil Elvis.*

Thank you... thank you very much.

Credits

Art Premiere erscheint achtmal jährlich bei mg/publishing/, Industriestr. 15, D-76437 Rastatt.
Internet: www.art-fantastix.de – E-Mail: redaktion@art-fantastix.de

Kunst / *Art* **Drew Posada**
Satz / *Set* & Layout **Oliver Marx**
Übersetzung / *Translation* **Gabriele Witz**
Redaktion / *Editor* **Frank Tuppi**
Chefredaktion / *Editor-in-chief* **Ralf Heinrich**

mg/publishing/ dankt Drew Posada für seine vertrauensvolle Zusammenarbeit.
mg/publishing/ would like to thank Drew Posada for his trusting cooperation.

Druck / *Printing:* Konradin Druck, Leinfelden-Echterdingen (Germany).
Vertrieb Fachhandel / *Distribution German special market:*
Modern Graphics Distribution, Lochfeldstr. 3o, 76437 Rastatt (Germany).
Vertrieb Presse / *German Distribution press:*
BPV Buch- und Pressevertrieb, Römerstr. 9o, 79618 Rheinfelden (Germany).

This edition courtesy of Fanfare, P.O. Box 617, Dagenham, RM8 1GD, England.

Co-published in North America by SQP Inc, 38 Rappleyea Rd - Howell, NJ o7731, U.S.A.
Visit our website! www.sqpinc.com

Distributed in Italy by Dream Colours srl - Lucca - Italy.

Vorwort

Es war im Frühjahr 2000 als ich das Vergnügen hatte, in die Kunst von Drew Posada eingeführt zu werden. Auf den ersten Blick war ich vom Stil und der Technik dieses jungen und aufstrebenden Talents fasziniert. Ich wußte in diesem Augenblick, daß er sich dazu entwikkeln würde, einer der talentiertesten Künstler auf dem Gebiet der Glamour und Pin-up Kunst dieser Generation zu werden. Seine Leidenschaft und der Elan, laufend Fortschritte zu machen und sich zu verbessern, war von Anfang an offensichtlich. Ich hatte nun das Vergnügen, seine Arbeit sich entfalten zu sehen und ihn bei der Entwicklung seines Stils und Technik, welche sein Markenzeichen ist, zu beobachten. Ich glaube nicht, daß es heutzutage noch einen Künstler gibt, der solch realistische Bilder wie Drew Posada mit Hilfe seiner Phantasie, Airbrush und eines Computers schaffen kann. Im 21. Jahrhundert muß man einsehen, daß Kunst sich auch weiterhin entwickeln wird und muß, wobei sie viele Drehungen und Wendungen mit jungen Künstlern nehmen wird, die neue Stile und innovative Techniken entwickeln. Dabei halten sie mit den stetigen Veränderungen unserer Gesellschaft und Technologie Schritt. Ich glaube Drew Posada ist ein Innovator, ein wahres Talent, der anderen jungen und talentierten Künstlern in zukünftigen Generationen den Weg zeigt, seinem Pfad zu folgen. Es war eine Ehre, mit Drew zu arbeiten. Und für all seine Fans und Bewunderer – davon bin ich überzeugt – steht er erst am Anfang von dem, was eine brilliante und hervorstechende Karriere als Künstler sein wird. Ich kann mit Gewißheit sagen, daß Drew Posada einen herausragenden Platz unter seinen Zeitgenossen als einer der innovativsten und talentiertesten Künstler dieses Jahrhunderts in der Welt des Pin-ups bekommen wird.

Foreword

It was in the spring of 2000 when I had the pleasure of being introduced to the Art of Drew Posada, at first glance I was fascinated by the style and technique of this young and emerging talent, it was at that very moment that I knew he would evolve to become one of this generations most talented artists in the genre of glamour and pinup art. His passion and drive to continuely improve and do better was obvious from the very start. I have now had the pleasure of seeing his work evolve and watch him develope his style and technique which is his own identity. I do not believe there is another artist today who can create such realistic images like Drew Posada can do withn the use of his imagination and an airbrush on a computer. In the 21st Century one must realize that art will and must continue to evolve taking many twists and turns with young artists developing new styles and innovative techniques, keeping up with the constant changes our society and technology. I believe Drew Posada is an innovator, a true talent leading the way for other young and talented artists in future generations to follow his path. It has been an honor to work with Drew and for all his fans and admirers he is only at the very beginning of what I am certain will be a brilliant and outstanding career as an artist. I can say with certainty that Drew Posada will hold a prominent place amongst his contempories as one of this centurys most innovative and talented artists in the World of Pinup.

Robert Steven Bane (Verleger/*publisher*)

Biographie

Von Drews bestem Freund und Schriftsteller, Joe Antonelli.
7. März 2002

Drews Annäherung an die Kunst spiegelt seine Haltung gegenüber allem anderen, was er im Leben tut, wider. Er ist auf der steten Suche nach Vervollkommnung – was er gestern gemacht hat, ist nicht so gut wie das, was er heute tun wird. Für Drew ist das Leben ein Wettstreit, und die Gewinner sind diejenigen, die nicht aufgeben, sondern fortfahren, ihre Ziele bis zum Ende zu verfolgen.

Paradoxerweise bin ich niemals jemandem begegnet, der nach außen hin so nicht-wettstreitend erscheint (mit Ausnahme von Viertelmeilen-Rennen und Tischtennis). Seine Wettbewerbsfähigkeit findet mit sich selbst statt und ist sehr wahrscheinlich die Folge des Aufwachsens mit seinem identischen Zwilling, Alex.
Wenn man Drew die Geschichte seiner Jugend erzählen hört, war Alex nicht ein identischer Zwilling mit identischen Genen. Alex war in allem besser (wenigstens in allem, was Drew interessierte) und von frühester Kindheit an setzte Alex die Maßstäbe, die Drew zu erreichen versuchte.

Mit einem talentierten Bruder aufzuwachsen, bedeutet: Alles war ein Wettstreit. Er konnte am schnellsten laufen, am zielsichersten schießen und – natürlich – am besten zeichnen. Dies waren die täglichen Maßstäbe, die Drew zu erreichen bemüht war (und immer noch ist).

Sein künstlerisches Talent wuchs schnell. Im Alter von sechzehn Jahren wurde er das erste Mal für seine Arbeit bezahlt. Aber, wie er oft erinnert wurde, war Kunst keine Möglichkeit, seinen Lebensunterhalt zu verdienen. Er entschloß sich, vorhergehend einen Kollegen zu besuchen, und rahmte nach der Highschool Gemälde. Trotz seines Könnens als Rahmer und der Kundschaft, die er sich aufbaute, war die Arbeit für den jungen Künstler eine Qual: die Arbeiten anderer Künstler gut aussehen zu lassen, war eine ständige Erinnerung an seine eigenen Wünsche. Schließlich mußte er der unausweichlichen Schlußfolgerung ins Auge sehen, daß die Kunst in seinem Blut lag und daß er niemals zufrieden sein würde, bis er nicht derjenige war, der sie schuf.

Ein Umzug von Seattle nach Südkalifornien brachte mehr als nur einen Wetterwechsel. Er wurde im Frühjahr '94 sofort von Image Comics engagiert und seine Arbeiten erschienen in den Comics von Top Cow, Wildstorm und Extreme Studios. Die Arbeit an Comics zwang Drew, seine Kunstfertigkeit zu verfeinern. Comics bewirkten auch eine Veränderung der Technik, die kaum ein Jahrzehnt früher unmöglich gewesen wäre: das Anwenden von Computer-Airbrush, der eine größere künstlerische Wendigkeit und Experimentieren erlaubte.

Drews Arbeit an Comics brachte ihm Zuspruch und ein angenehmes Leben ein, aber er sehnte sich danach, für seine Pin-up-Kunst anerkannt zu werden. Während er seine Technik verfeinern wollte, war es die Arbeit der beiden Legenden des Pin-up, Sorayama und Olivia, die für Drew wirklich die Blockade aufhoben. Und ihm war klar, daß er, um es auf dem Gebiet der Pin-up-Kunst zu etwas zu bringen, bei Robert Bane Editions (die Tamara Bane Galerie in Los Angeles, Kalifornien) gewesen sein mußte. Hochtrabende Ziele. Die Bane Galerie stellte bereits Sorayama und Olivia aus, und als Drew das erste Mal versuchte, dort ausgestellt zu werden, riet man ihm, seine Kunstfertigkeit zu verfeinern. Für die meisten Künstler wäre die das Aus gewesen, aber Drew hatte ein klares Ziel, und seine Wettbewerbsinstinkte wurden entfacht.

Er ging an die Arbeit zurück, konzentrierte sich auf Details, entfaltete seine Kunstfertigkeit, verzichtete auf das bequeme Leben mit Comics. Er hatte eine Berufung, eine, der er sich nicht entziehen konnte ohne seine Daseinsberechtigung aufzugeben. Zwei Jahre vergingen, und als er Robert Bane seine neuen Arbeiten vorlegte, wurde er enthusiastisch begrüßt und in die Galerie aufgenommen.

Was Sie auf den folgenden Seiten sehen, zeigt seine neuesten Arbeiten; und dennoch sollten diese Bilder als die erste Phase eines reifen Künstlers angesehen werden. Sie sind Vorboten für bessere Dinge, die kommen werden: Als Künstler und als Mensch ist Drew immer noch im Wettstreit mit sich selbst, noch immer experimentierend und seine Kunstfertigkeit und neue Ausdrucksmöglichkeiten entwickelnd, denn der kleinere Zwilling steckt noch immer in ihm.

Während Drews Karriere weitergeht, sehen Sie sich nach Drews Kunst um, die neue Perspektiven bringt, die Pin-up, wie sie heute ist, übertrifft und die seine Entdeckungsreise fortführt.

Biography

By Drew's best friend and writer Joe Antonelli.
March 7, 2002

Drew's approach to art reflects his attitude toward everything else he does in life. He is on a constant quest for improvement: what he did yesterday is not as good as what he will do today. For Drew, life is a competition, and the winners are those who do not give up, but continue to pursue their goals to the end.

Paradoxically, I have never encountered anyone who is outwardly as non-competitive as Drew (with the exceptions of standing quarter mile times and ping pong). His competitiveness is with himself, most likely the result of growing up with an identical twin, Alex.

To hear Drew tell the story of his youth, Alex was not an identical twin with identical genes. Alex was better at everything (at least everything Drew was interested in) and from an early age, Alex set the benchmarks which Drew would try to achieve.

Growing up with a talented brother meant everything was a competition. Who could run fastest, shoot straightest, and of course, draw best: these were the daily marks Drew strove to achieve (and still does).

His talent for art grew quickly: by the age of sixteen, he was being paid for his work. But as he was often reminded, art was no way to make a living. He chose to forego college, and went to work after high school as a picture framer. Despite his skill as a framer and the clientele he developed, the work was torture for the young artist: making other artists' works look great was a constant reminder of his own desires. Finally, he had to face the inescapable conclusion that art was in his blood, and that he would never be satisfied unless he was the one creating.

A move from Seattle to Southern California brought more than a change of weather. He was hired immediately by Image Comics in spring of '94, and his work appeared in the comic books of Top Cow, Wildstorm and Extreme Studios.

Working in comics forced Drew to hone his craft. Comics also brought about a change in technique that would not have been possible even a decade earlier: the use of a computer airbrush, which allows for greater artistic flexibility and experimentation.

Drew's work in comics won him acclaim and a decent living, but he yearned to be recognized for his pinup art. While he wanted to improve his technique, it was the work of the two legends of pinup, Sorayama and Olivia, who truly raised the bar for Drew. And he knew that in order to have made it in the field of pinup art, he had to be at Robert Bane Editions (the Tamara Bane Gallery in Los Angeles, California). Lofty goals. The Bane Gallery already represented Sorayama and Olivia, and when Drew first attempted to be represented there, he was told to improve his craft. For most artists, that would be the kiss of death, but for Drew, it gave him a clear goal, and his competitive instincts were rekindled.

He went back to work, focusing on the details, developing his craft, sacrificing his comfortable living with comics. He was on a mission, one that he could not turn away from without giving up his reason for being. Two years passed, and when he submitted his new work to Robert Bane, he was greeted enthusiastically and welcomed to the gallery.

What you see on the following pages reflects his most recent works, and yet these paintings should be viewed as the first phase of a mature artist. These are a precursor to better things to come: as an artist and a person, Drew is still in competition with himself, still experimenting and developing his craft and new ways of expression, for the smaller twin has never left him.

As his career continues, look for Drew's art to bring new perspectives, to transcend where pinup is today, and to continue his journey of discovery.

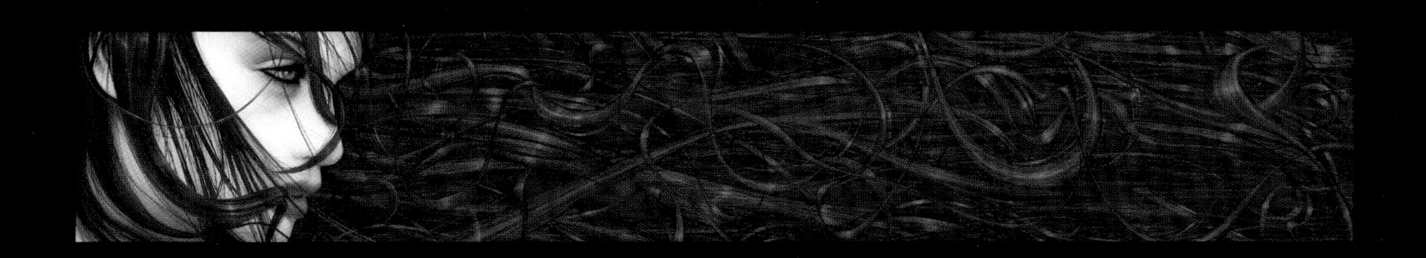

Drew Posada

Drew unter dem Einfluß von...

Simon „Biz" Bisley – Meiner Meinung nach malt er die männliche Figur besser als irgendein anderer der Geschichte. Große Worte, wenn man all die großartigen Künstler bedenkt.

Hajime Sorayama – Er malt Frauen besser als irgendein anderer der Geschichte, und er ist „der" Meistertechniker.

Frank Frazetta – Er beherrscht die männliche *und* die weibliche Figur und verleiht seiner Kunst Leben wie kein anderer, *und* er war schon ein Meister, als all die großartigen heutigen Künstler noch Kinder oder nicht einmal geboren waren, deshalb... er ist meiner Meinung nach der beste Künstler von allen in der Geschichte der Menschheit. Bei weitem mein größter Einfluß während ich heranwuchs. Er *ist* eine lebende Legende.

Olivia de Berardinis – Ihr Gespür für Stil und ihre Ideen bei ihren Pin-ups sind sehr sinnlich und schöpferisch. Sie mischt Realität mit Spaß und Sexualität wie es niemand sonst getan hat. Man findet dieses Talent sehr selten bei einem Künstler. Ihre Werke scheinen zu vermitteln, daß sie Spaß beim Malen hatte. Ich hoffe, etwas davon eines Tages in meiner Arbeit einzufangen.

Ebenso zählen zu meinen Favoriten: Sir Lawrence Alma-Tadema, William Bouguereau, J.C. Leyendecker, Normal Rockwell, Tom Lovell, Joe Chiodo, Sam Liu und all die alten Pin-up Künstler der alten Schule wie Elvgren, Petty, Vargas, etc...

Drew under the Influence of...

Simon "Biz" Bisley – *In my opinion he paints the male form better than anyone else in history. Mighty tall order considering all the great artists.*

Hajime Sorayama – *He paints women better than anyone else in history, and he is "the" master technician.*

Frank Frazetta – *He's mastered the male* and *female form and lends a life to his art like no other,* and *was a master when all the great artists today were still kids or not even born yet, therefore... he is the best artist of all in the history of mankind, in my opinion. By far my biggest influence growing up. He* is *a living legend.*

Olivia de Berardinis – *Her sense of style and her ideas in her pinups are very sensual and creative, she mixes reality with fun and sexuality like no one else has. It's very rare to find these qualities in any artist. Her pieces seem to convey that she had a fun time painting them. I hope to someday capture some of that in my work.*

Also among my favorites: Sir Lawrence Alma-Tadema, William Bouguereau, J.C. Leyendecker, Normal Rockwell, Tom Lovell, Joe Chiodo, Sam Liu, and all the old school pinup artists like Elvgren, Petty, Vargas, etc...

Technik

Viele Menschen sind neugierig, wie ich meine Bilder schaffe und male. Es ist nicht so kompliziert, wie man vielleicht denkt. Als erstes fertige ich eine Zeichnumg des Pin-ups an. Dies dauert irgendwo zwischen ein paar Stunden bis zu ein paar Tagen, abhängig davon, wie ausgearbeitet der Hintergrund ausfällt und ähnliches. Dann, wenn ich mit dem Bild zufrieden bin, scanne ich es mit dem Bildbearbeitungsprogramm Adobe Photoshop in meinen Computer und beginne, es zu brushen. Ich zeichne auf einem druckempfindlichen Wacom-Tablett. Je stärker ich mit der Feder auf das Tablett drücke, desto mehr Tusche kommt aus der Airbrush des Programms. Die Menschen sind immer neugierig, wie ich die Haare male. Alles, was ich tue, ist, eine „Ein-Pixel-Bürste" zu benutzen und stundenlang Haare zu kreieren. Es dauert sehr lange und ist sehr ermüdend, aber die Ergebnisse sind es wert. Entgegen der Meinung einiger Leute manipuliere ich *keine* Fotos oder benutze 3-D-Programme. Ich „male" die Pin-ups 100% mit Adobe Photoshop. Ich vermisse das Malen von Bildern mit richtiger Farbe und Leinwand, deshalb habe ich vor, in Zukunft mehr Originalgemälde zu erstellen.

Technique

Many people are curious as to how I go about creating and painting my images. It's not as complicated as people might think. The first thing I do is to make a drawing of the pinup. This takes anywhere from a couple of hours to a couple of days, depending on how elaborate the background ends up being and things like that. Then, when I'm happy with the drawing I'll scan it into my computer using a painting program called Adobe Photoshop and paint it using the airbrush. I use a pressure sensitive Wacom tablet to paint on. The harder I press on the tablet with the pen the more ink comes out of the airbrush in the paint program. People are always curious as to how I paint the hair. All I do is use a "one pixel brush" and create hair for hours, it takes a long time and is very tedious, but the results are worth it. Contrary to what some people believe I do not *manipulate photos or use 3-D programs. I "paint" the pinups 100% in Adobe Photoshop. I do miss painting images with actual paint and boards, so I plan on doing more original paintings in the future.*

DREW ©'99

DREW © '99

DREW
ALEX

DREW ©'00

HARD SCRATCHES AND KNICKS ON BLADE

DREW
©'00

DREW
© '00

DREW ©'99

DREW ©'99

DREW
©'00

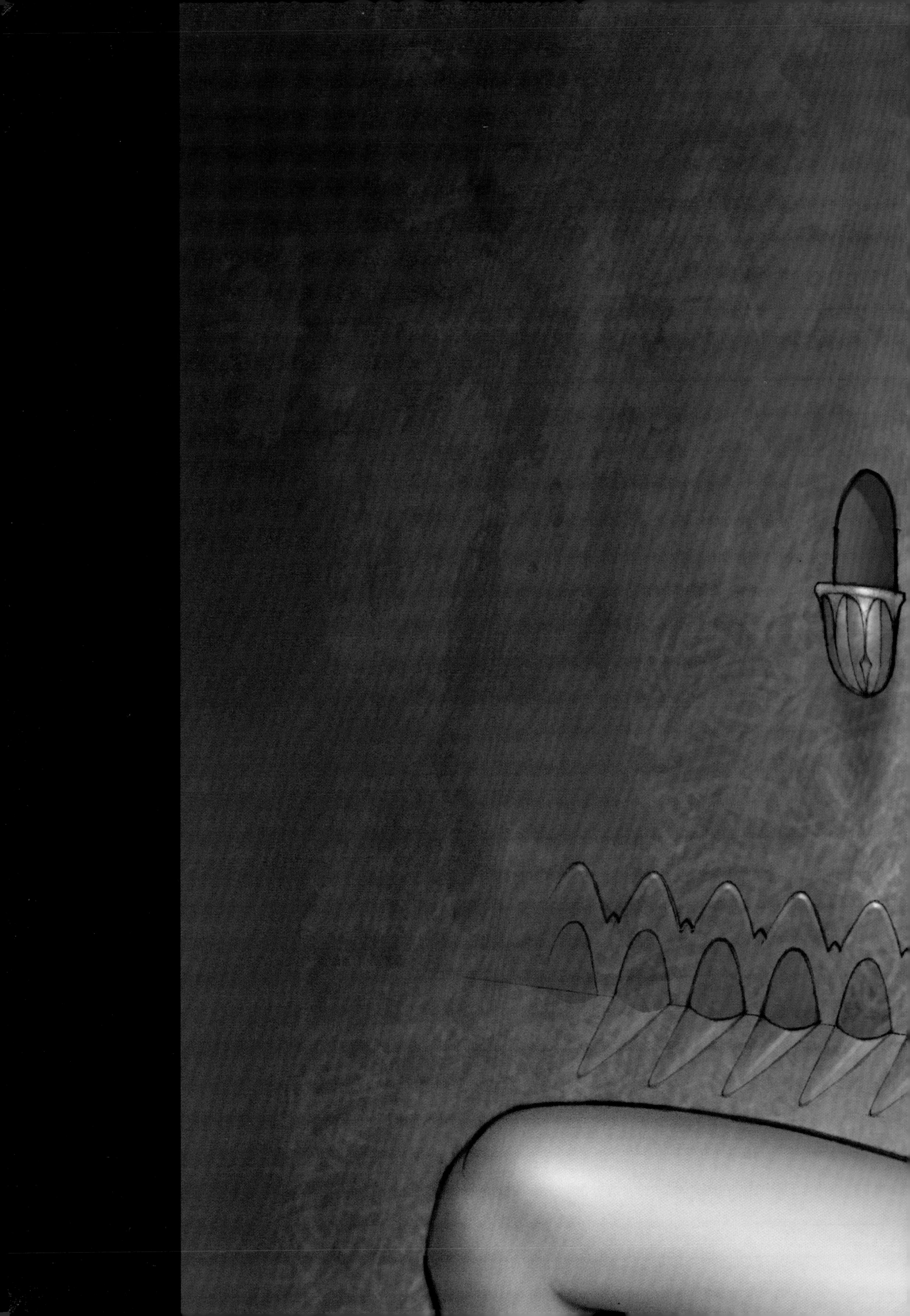

6
3
8

·DREW· © '01

DREW ©'99

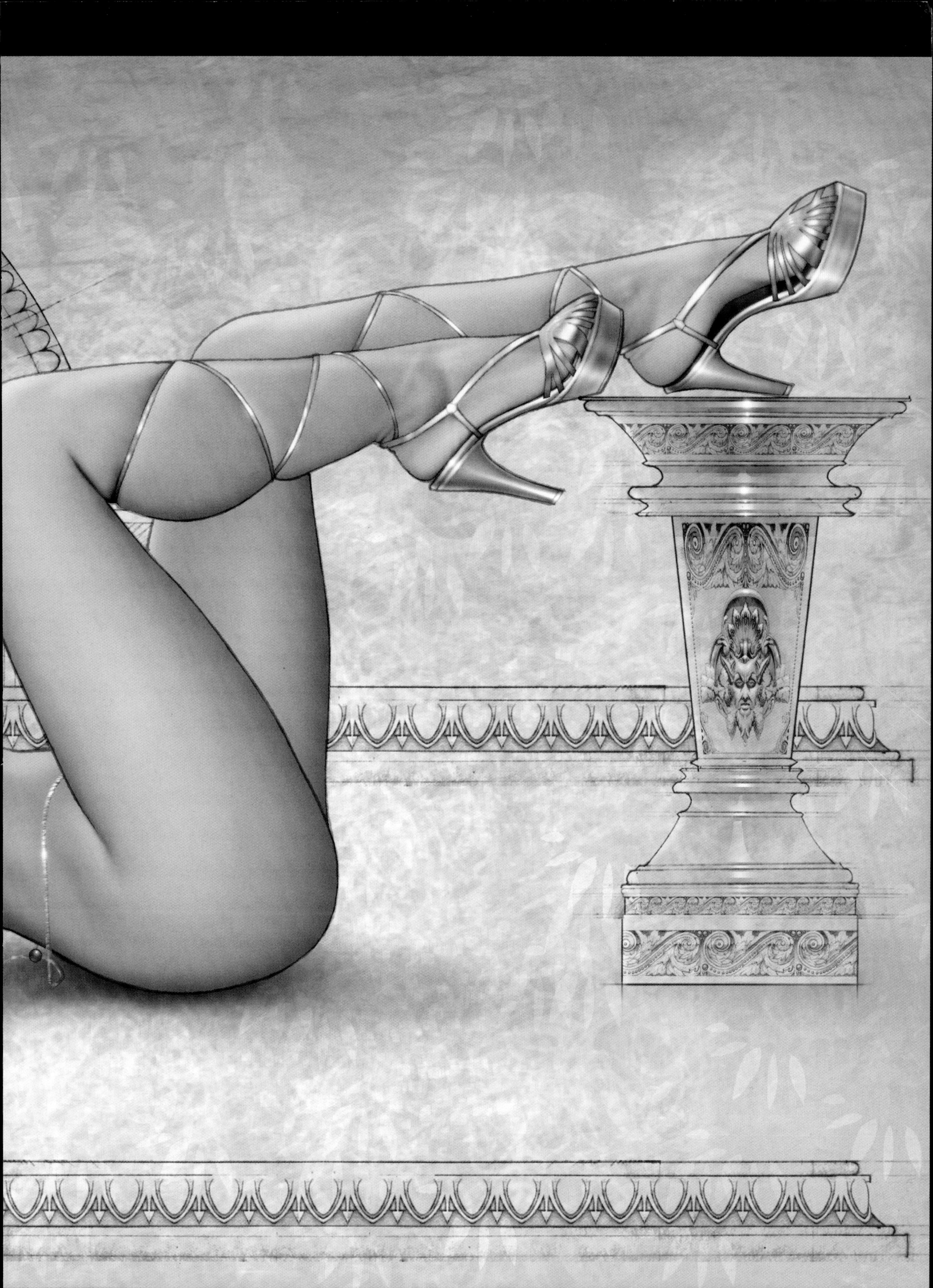

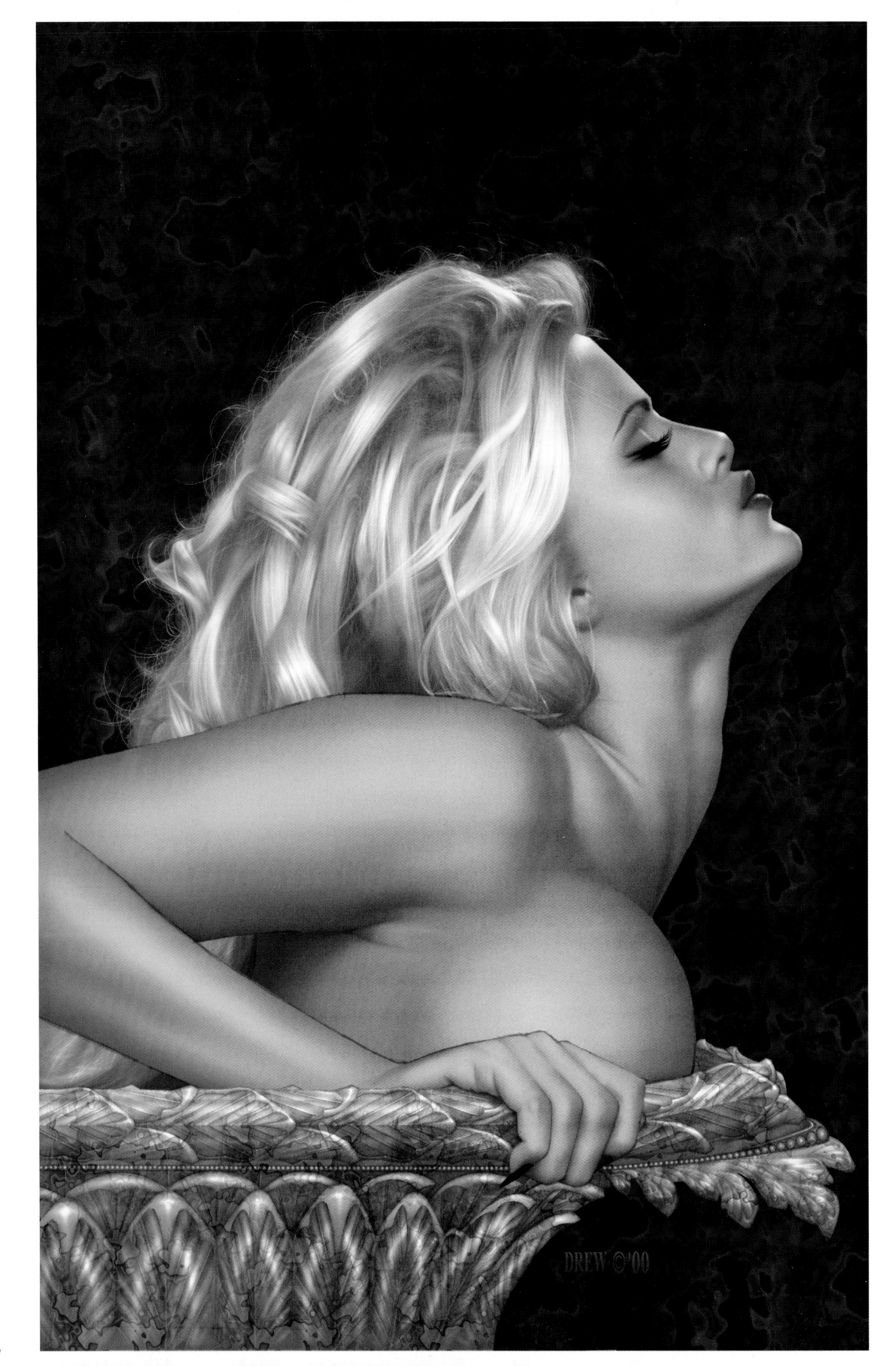
DREW ©'00

INDEX

Seite/Page 8
Blade (1997)

Seite/Page 9
Jester (2002)

53,3x81,3cm / 21“x32“

Dies ist das dritte Bild innerhalb einer Serie von Drucken von Suzi Simpson (www.suzisimpson.tv).

This is the third image in a series of editions of Suzi Simpson (www.suzisimpson.tv).

Seite/Page 10
X'alpen

Diese erste Version wurde als eine Halloween-Sammelkarte benutzt, verlegt von Verotik. © Verotik.

This first version was used as a Halloween collector card published by Verotik. © Verotik.

Seite/Page 11
Pumpkin Pie (1998)

Dieses Bild ist eine limitierte Auflage von Robert Bane Editions, Los Angeles, Kalifornien, und der Tamara Bane Galerie (www.worldofpinup.com).

This image is a limited edition through Robert Bane Editions of Los Angeles, California, and The Tamara Bane Gallery (www.worldofpinup.com).

Seite/Page 12
Venus (1998)

Dieses Bild wurde als Titelbild für ein Pin-up Comic mit dem Namen Venus DoMina benutzt; verlegt von Verotik.

This image was used as a cover for a pinup comic book called Venus DoMina, published by Verotik.

Seite/Page 13
9 Shark (1999)

Dieses war das erste von vielen Bildern, um die Aufmerksamkeit von Robert Bane zu erlangen, und wurde mein erster limitierter Druck bei der Tamara Bane Galerie. Das Modell ist Jana.

This was the first of my images to get the attention of Robert Bane and became the first limited edition for me through the Tamara Bane Gallery. The model's name is Jana.

Seite/Page 14
Queen's Knight (1999)

Dieses ist ebenfalls ein limitierter Druck von Robert Bane, und ich benutzte dasselbe Modell, Jana. Ich wurde durch den Besitzer eines lokalen Zigarrengeschäfts (Max Amar, Orange/Kalifornien) inspiriert. Amar macht regelmäßig jeden fertig, der aufzusteigen wünscht und sein Glück bei einer freundschaftlichen Partie Schach versucht.

This is also a limited edition through Robert Bane and I used the same model, Jana. I was inspired by the owner of a local cigar shop (Max Amar, Orange, CA). Amar regularly destroys anyone who wishes to step up and try their fate at a friendly game of chess.

Seite/Page 15
Jinn (1999)

Dieses Bild wurde als Titelbild für einen Comic des gleichen Namens benutzt; verlegt von Avalon Studios. Ich benutzte Jana als Modellvorlage.

This image was used as a cover of a comic book of the same name published by Avalon Studios. I used Jana as a model reference.

Seite/Page 16
Séance (2000)

Auftrag von Kirk Dilbeck, eine seiner Figuren als limitierte Auflage durch Artis Studios zu malen. „Séance“ © und ™ Kirk Dilbeck.

Commissioned by Kirk Dilbeck to paint one of his characters as a limited edition through Artis studios. "Séance" © and ™ Kirk Dilbeck.

Seite/Page 17
Wicked (1999)

Auch als Comic-Titelbild für ein Comic gleichen Namens benutzt, verlegt durch Avalon Studios. Auch hierfür war Jana das Modell.

Also used as a comic book cover for a comic book of the same name, published through Avalon Studios. Jana was the model for this as well.

Seite/Page 18/19
Red (2000)

Von Brian Haberlin von Avalon Studios als limitierte Auflage in Auftrag gegeben.

Commissioned by Brian Haberlin of Avalon Studios as a limited edition.

Seite/Page 20
Slayer (2001)

Auftrag von Robert Bane, „Demonslayer“ auf eine erotischere Art für eine limitierte Auflage zu verändern.

Commissioned by Robert Bane to alter "Demonslayer" in a more erotic fashion for a limited edition.

Seite/Page 21
Angela (1999)

Keines meiner prächtigsten Bilder. Eigentlich begann es mein Zwillingsbruder Alex, und ich beendete es. Ich glaube es wurde für ein Comic-Titelbild für ein Buch mit dem Titel „The Wicked“ benutzt, verlegt durch Avalon Studios, exklusiv für Tower Records. „Angela“ © und ™ Todd McFarlane.

Not one of my proudest images. Actually, my twin brother Alex started it and I finished it. I think it was used for a comic book cover for a book called "The Wicked" published through Avalon Studios as an exclusive through Tower Records. "Angela" © and ™ Todd McFarlane.

Seite/Page 22
Blossommm (2000)

Limitierte Auflage der Tamara Bane Galerie. Das Modell war Jana.

Limited edition through The Tamara Bane Gallery. The model used is Jana.

Seite/Page 23
Broadhead (2000)

Im Comic „The Wicked“ als Pin-up veröffentlicht.

Published inside "The Wicked" comic book as a pinup.

Seite/Page 24/25
High Heels (2000)

Von Verleger Robert Bane als limitierte Auflage in Auftrag gegeben. Als Vorlage benutzte ich die Skizze einer der besten Bleistiftzeichner in der Geschichte der Comics und einer der besten Zeichner, die ich jemals getroffen habe... Sam Liu. Seine Zeichnung war genial und paßte zu der Beschreibung dessen, wonach Robert Bane suchte. Also zeichnete ich seine Skizze neu und benutzte sie. Das ist der Grund, warum ich Sam die Lorbeeren zu Teil werden lassen möchte. Sehen Sie einige seiner unglaublichen Arbeiten unter: www.itchstudios.com

Commissioned by publisher Robert Bane as a limited edition. For reference I used the sketch of one of the best pencilers in the history of comic books and one of the best illustrators I've ever met... Sam Liu. His drawing was genius and it fit in the description of what Robert Bane was looking for, so I redrew his sketch and used it, and that's why I want to give Sam the credit. Check out some of his amazing work at: www.itchstudios.com

Seite/Page 26
Dawn (2000)

Das ist meine wunderbare Freundin, Dawn. Dieses Bild ist eines meiner Lieblingsbilder, und ich verwandte mehr Zeit und Energie auf dieses Bild als auf jedes andere bis zu diesem Zeitpunkt. Es ist eines meiner prächtigsten Werke. Es wurde als Titelbild für ein Comic mit dem Titel „The Wicked“ benutzt.

This is my wonderful girlfriend, Dawn. This image is one of my favorites and I spent more time and energy on this image than any other up to this point. It's one of my proudest accomplishments. It was used as a cover on a comic book called "The Wicked."

Seite/Page 27
Statue (2000)

Bis jetzt noch nie gedruckt oder benutzt.

Never printed or used until now.

Seite/Page 28
Medusa (2000)

Von Brian Habelin von Avalon Studios in Auftrag gegeben, um als Titelbild für den Comic mit dem Titel „The Wicked“ benutzt zu werden. Als Vorlage für einige Haare der Figur benutzte ich meinen großen schwarzen Tausendfüßler aus Tansania. Sein Name war Lil' Bastard.

Commissioned by Brian Haberlin of Avalon Studios to be used as a cover for the comic book "The Wicked." I used my Giant Black Tanzanian Millipede as reference for some of the creature's hair. His name was Lil' Bastard.

Seite/Page 29
Vampyre (2000)

Benutzt als Titelbild für einen Comic mit dem Titel „The Wicked“.

Used as a cover for a comic book called "The Wicked."

Seite/Page 3o/31

Aria/Angela (1999)

Diese beiden Bilder waren für ein Crossover zwischen diesen beiden Comicfiguren vorgesehen, aber es wurde niemals realisiert. Brian Haberlin, CEO der Avalan Studios, beschloß, die linke Hälfte für das Titelbild eines Comics mit dem Titel „Aria" zu benutzen. „Angela" © und ™ Todd McFarlane.

These two images were supposed to be for a crossover between these two comic book characters, but it never happened. Brian Haberlin, CEO of Avalon Studios, ended up using the left half for a cover on a comic book called "Aria." "Angela" © and ™ Todd McFarlane.

Seite/Page 32

Samurai (2ooo)

Variante zu „Tamara". Es wurde bis heute niemals veröffentlicht.

Alternate version to "Tamara." It's never been published until now.

Seite/Page 33

Tamara (2ooo)

Dies war ein Auftrag von Verleger Robert Bane, seine Frau Tamara für eine limitierte Auflage zu malen.

This was a commission from publisher Robert Bane to paint his wife, Tamara, as a limited edition.

Seite/Page 34/35

Mardi Gras (2oo2)

Bis heute unveröffentlicht. Dies ist eines meiner Favoriten. Ich verwandte viel Zeit und Energie darauf, und ich erlaubte mir ein bißchen mehr Spaß als gewöhnlich. Ich glaube, deshalb war niemand daran interessiert, es zu veröffentlichen. Ich malte dieses Mädchen nach Mardi Gras, ohne ihr Kostüm, nur mit ihrem Kopfschmuck, und es erschien mir irgendwie faszinierend. Das Modell ist wieder einmal... genau! Sie haben es erraten, Jana.

Never published until now. This is one of my favorites. I spent a lot of time and energy on this one and I let myself have a little more fun than I usually do. I think that's why nobody was interested in publishing it. I pictured this girl after Mardi Gras with her costume off except for her head dress, and it seemed kind of intriguing to me. The model is, once again...yep! You guessed it, Jana.

Seite/Page 36

Whipped (2oo1)

76,2x5o,8cm / 3o"x2o"
Prismacolor on board.

Verkauft durch die Tamara Bane Galerie. Das Modell war Jana.

Sold through The Tamara Bane Gallery. Jana was the model.

Seite/Page 37

Moonshine (2oo1)

5o,8x38,1cm / 2o"x15"
Oil Pastel on board.

Verkauft durch die Tamara Bane Galerie. Das Modell war Julie Strain.

Sold through The Tamara Bane Gallery. Julie Strain was the model.

Seite/Page 38

8 Ball (2oo1)

Auftrag von Robert Bane als limitierte Auflage durch die Tamara Bane Galerie. Eine der schönsten Frauen der Welt stand Modell für dieses Stück. Ihr Name ist Aria Giovanni.

Commissioned by Robert Bane as a limited edition through The Tamara Bane Gallery. One of the most beautiful women in the world was the model for this piece; her name is Aria Giovanni.

Seite/Page 39

Queen of Pain (2oo1)

Von einem der coolsten Typen im Verlagsgeschäft, Kevin Easterman, als Titelbild für eine Ausgabe von „Heavy Metal" veröffentlicht. Ich glaube, für die Ausgabe Mai 2oo2.

Being published by one of the coolest guys in publishing, Kevin Easterman, for a cover of Heavy Metal magazine. I think the May issue of 2oo2.

Seite/Page 4o

Vampirella (2oo1)

Ich malte diese Variante von „8 Ball" in der Hoffnung, ein Titelbild bei Harris Comics zu bekommen. Aber sie waren nicht sonderlich interessiert. Bis jetzt war es noch nie gedruckt zu sehen. „Vampirella" © und ™ Harris Comics.

I painted this variant of „8 Ball" in hopes of getting a cover at Harris Comics, but they weren't too interested. It's never seen print until now. "Vampirella" © and ™ Harris Comics.

Seite/Page 41

Heaven & Hell (1999)

Benutzt als Titelbild für einen Comic mit dem Titel „The Wicked", verlegt durch Avalon Studios und exklusiv durch Tower Records.

Used as a cover for a comic book called "The Wicked" published through Avalon Studios and was an exclusive through Tower Records.

Seite/Page 42/43

Suzi (2oo2)

Auftrag von Verleger Robert Bane als das erste von sechs Bildern, die als limitierte Auflage durch die Tamara Bane Galerie (www.worldofpinup.com) verkauft werden sollten.

Commissioned by publisher Robert Bane as the first of six images to be sold as limited editions through The Tamara Bane Gallery (www.worldofpinup.com).

Seite/Page 44

Kiss (2ooo)

Im Comic „The Wicked" als Pin-up veröffentlicht.

Published in "The Wicked" comic book as a pinup.

Seite/Page 45

Top Hat (2oo2)

Auftrag von Verleger Robert Bane als das zweite von sechs Bildern, die als limitierte Auflage durch die Tamara Bane Galerie (www.worldofpinup.com) verkauft werden sollten.

Commissioned by publisher Robert Bane as the second of six images to be sold as limited editions through The Tamara Bane Gallery (www.worldofpinup.com).

www.artofdrew.com

Die offizielle Website von Drew Posada war zum Redaktionsschluß noch nicht fertig, aber geplant sind eine Galerie mit all seinen Werken, Bestellmöglichkeit diverser Drucke und Lithographien, ein Bereich mit den Antworten auf häufig gestellte Fragen, Informationen zu den Arbeitstechniken sowie eine Karriereübersicht mit Biographie und Zukunftsplänen. Außerdem gibt es die üblichen Links zu anderen interessanten Websites und seinen Models. Auch ein direkter E-Mail-Kontakt ist mit Drew über seine Website möglich. Übrigens ist auch ein Bereich geplant, in dem seine schon oft nachgefragten Comic-Arbeiten zu sehen sind, die einen großen Teil seines bisherigen Schaffens ausmachen. Eine vielversprechende Site also, die sicher einen Besuch lohnt.

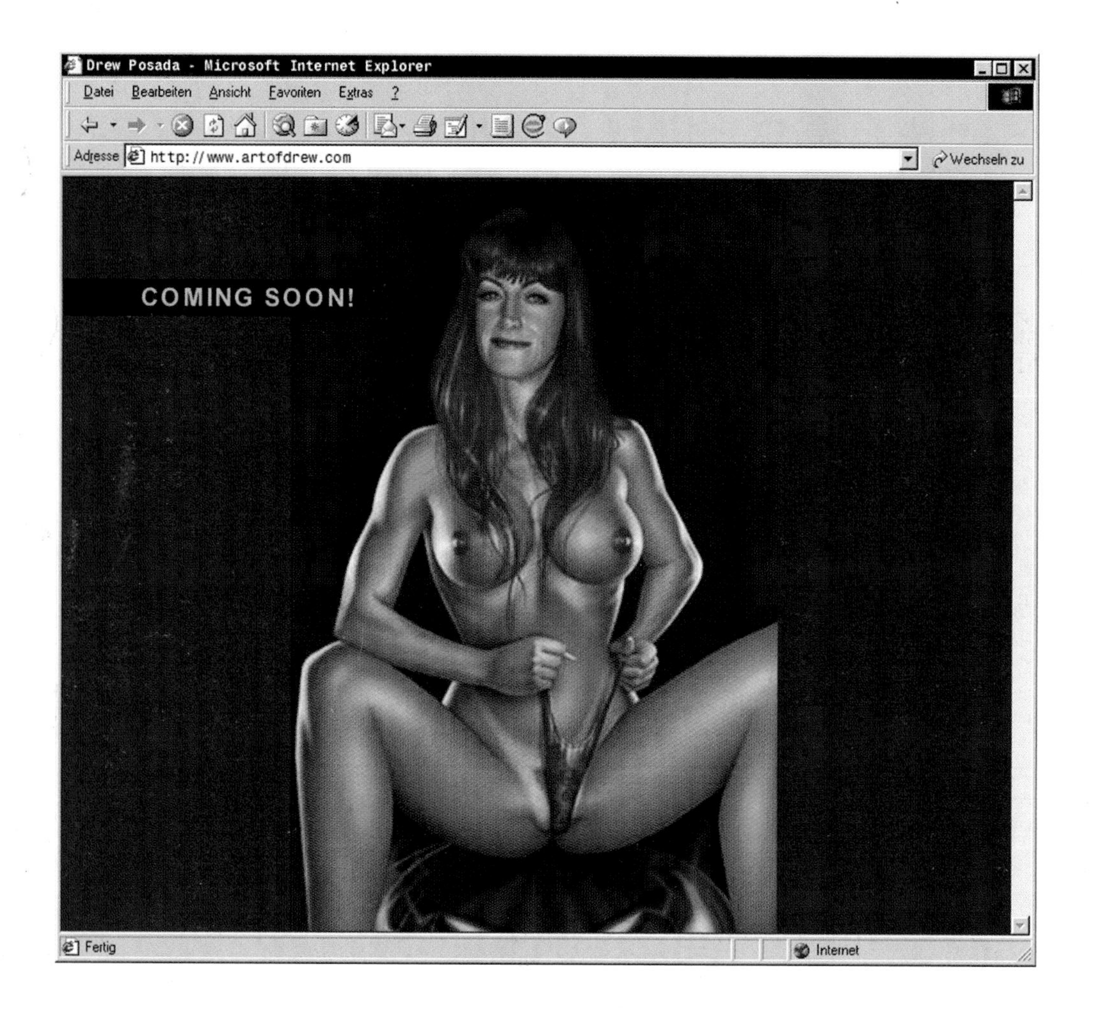

The official web site of Drew Posada has not been finished at copy deadline. Howver, it is planned to present a galery with all of his works, a mail order for various prints and lithos, a section with answers to Frequently Asked Questions, information about his technique as well as a history section with a bio and forwards and such. Furthermore the usual links to other web sites of interest along with such to his models. Besides a section is planned, in which his comic works can be seen, for which many fans have been asking for a long time, since comics made up a large part of his previous works. Also featured is a direct e-mail contact to Drew. A very promising site, which pays a visit.